A YOUNG LION LIBRARY BOOK

A Children's Zoo

A YOUNG LION POETRY BOOK

An anthology of animal verse
chosen by

JULIA WATSON

A Children's Zoo

Illustrated by Karen Strachey

Young Lions
An Imprint of HarperCollinsPublishers

First published in Great Britain in Young Lions 1978
Fifth impression February 1993

Young Lions is an imprint of
HarperCollins Children's Books,
part of HarperCollins Publishers Ltd,
77–85 Fulham Palace Road,
Hammersmith, London W6 8JB

ISBN 0 00 671421-8

Printed and bound in Great Britain by
HarperCollins Manufacturing, Glasgow

A Children's Zoo

Six Feet and More
Spider – Alan Brownjohn   11
The Butterfly That Stamped – Rudyard Kipling   12
The Scorpion – Hilaire Belloc   13
On the Grasshopper and Cricket – John Keats   14
Way Down South – Traditional American   15
A centipede – Anonymous   16
Only my Opinion – Monica Shannon   17
Fireflies in the Garden – Robert Frost   18
the honey bee – Don Marquis   19
The Centipede – Carmen Bernos de Gasztold   20
The Dragon-Fly – Alfred, Lord Tennyson   21
The Tickle Rhyme – Ian Serraillier   22
Bee – George Barker   23
Butterfly – D. H. Lawrence   24
Bees in August – Roy Fuller   25

Four Feet
Furry Bear – A. A. Milne   28
Cats – Eleanor Farjeon   30
An Otter – Ted Hughes   31
Cows – James Reeves   32
The Monster – Edward Lowbry   34
Team of Oxen – Louis Untermeyer   35
The Runaway – Robert Frost   36
The Rhinoceros – Ogden Nash   37
Cat – J. R. R. Tolkien   38
A Sheep Fair – Thomas Hardy   40
Hedgehog – Miles Gibson   42

The Tin Frog – Russell Hoban   43
The Dog – Ogden Nash   44
The Pig – Spike Milligan   45
The Hippopotamus – Jack Prelutsky   46
The King – Douglas Livingstone   47
The Toads' Chorus – Rumer Godden   48
The Yak – Hilaire Belloc   50
The Mad Yak – Gregory Corso   51
The Galloping Cat – Stevie Smith   52
Alligator – Spike Milligan   55
Soliloquy of a Tortoise – E. V. Rieu   56
The Toaster – William Jay Smith   57
Earthy Anecdote – Wallace Stevens   58
Giraffe – Carson McCullers   59

Two Feet
The Ostrich – Ogden Nash   63
The Blackbird – Humbert Wolfe   64
The Silver Swan – Anonymous   65
The Eagle – Alfred, Lord Tennyson   66
The Mirror – A. A. Milne   67
The Bat – Theodore Roethke   68
The Red Cockatoo – Po Chu-I   70
The Sparrowhawk – Russell Hoban   71
The Caged Bird in Springtime – James Kirkup   72
The Cock – William Wordsworth   74
The Crow – Russell Hoban   75
The Duck – Ogden Nash   76

. . . and none
Snail – John Drinkwater   79
The Serpent – Theodore Roethke   80
Seal Lullaby – Rudyard Kipling   82
The Guppy – Ogden Nash   84
Worms and the Wind – Carl Sandburg   85

lines from Pike – Ted Hughes   86
The Sailor and the Seal – Rumer Godden   88

. . . and man
Wilderness – Carl Sandburg   90

Index of Authors and Poems   93

Six Feet and More

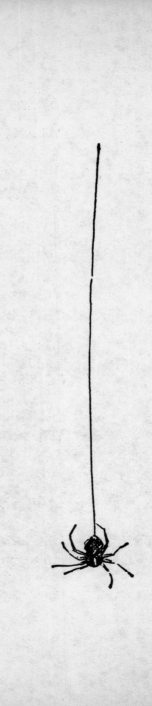

Spider

ALAN BROWNJOHN

I am a spider spinning down
from a beam
in a barn
near a little town
in a part of Northern Italy.
Circling happily, I can see
(past idle
dust-specks
in the air)
four hessian sacks and
half a chair
and lumps of farm
machinery.
One hour I have
been spinning down,
One hour I have been
circling round.
When I have finished I
will have spun
(invisibly and quietly)
one
thread from the ceiling
to the ground.

The Butterfly That Stamped

RUDYARD KIPLING

There was never a Queen like Balkis,
From here to the wide world's end;
But Balkis talked to a butterfly
As you would talk to a friend.

There was never a King like Solomon,
Not since the world began;
But Solomon talked to a butterfly
As a man would talk to a man.

She was the Queen of Sabaea,
And *he* was Asia's Lord –
But they both of 'em talked to butterflies
When they took their walks abroad!

The Scorpion

HILAIRE BELLOC

The Scorpion is as black as soot,
He dearly loves to bite;
He is a most unpleasant brute
To find in bed at night.

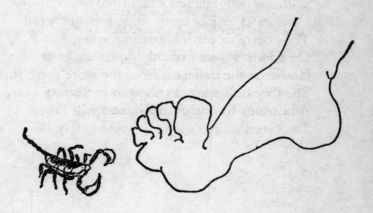

On the Grasshopper and Cricket

JOHN KEATS

The poetry of earth is never dead:
When all the birds are faint with the hot sun,
And hide in cooling trees, a voice will run
From hedge to hedge about the new-mown mead;
That is the Grasshopper's – he takes his lead
In summer luxury – he has never done
With his delights; for when tired out with fun
He rests at ease beneath some pleasant weed.
The poetry of earth is ceasing never:
On a lone winter evening, when the frost
Has wrought a silence, from the store there shrills
The Cricket's song, in warmth increasing ever,
And seems to one in drowsiness half lost,
The Grasshopper's among some grassy hill.

Way Down South

TRADITIONAL AMERICAN

Way down South where bananas grow,
A grasshopper stepped on an elephant's toe.
The elephant said, with tears in his eyes,
"Pick on somebody your own size."

A *centipede*

ANONYMOUS

A centipede was happy quite,
Until a frog in fun
Said, "Pray, which leg comes after which?"
This raised her mind to such a pitch,
She lay distracted in the ditch
Considering how to run.

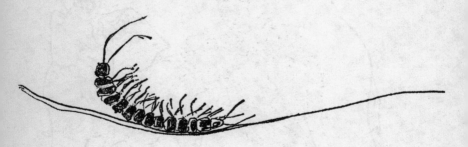

Only my Opinion

MONICA SHANNON

Is a caterpillar ticklish?
   Well, it's always my belief
That he giggles, as he wiggles
   Across a hairy leaf.

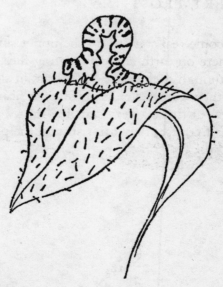

Fireflies in the Garden

ROBERT FROST

Here come real stars to fill the upper skies,
And here on earth come emulating flies,
That though they never equal stars in size,
(And they were never really stars at heart)
Achieve at times a very star-like start.
Only, of course, they can't sustain the part.

the honey bee

DON MARQUIS

the honey bee is sad and cross
and wicked as a weasel
and when she perches on you boss
she leaves a little measle.

The Centipede

CARMEN BERNOS DE GASZTOLD

from The Beasts' Choir, *translated by Rumer Godden*

With innumerable little footsteps
I go through life
but, Lord,
I can never
get to the end of myself!
It's a queer sensation
to be a multitude
that follows itself
in Indian file!
True,
it's the first step that counts
or, rather,
the first foot.
All that matters
is to be in step
with one's self:
I only ask,
Lord,
to jog along
one in spirit
without troublesome
reticences.

Amen.

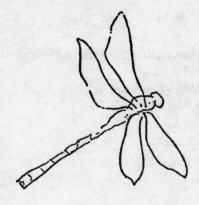

The Dragon-Fly

ALFRED, LORD TENNYSON

To-day I saw the dragon-fly
Come from the wells where he did lie.

An inner impulse rent the veil
of his old husk: from head to tail
Came out clean plates of sapphire mail.

He dried his wings: like gauze they grew;
Thro' crofts and pastures wet with dew
A living flash of light he flew.

The Tickle Rhyme

IAN SERRAILLIER

"Who's that tickling my back?" said the wall.
"Me," said a small
  caterpillar. "I'm learning
  to crawl."

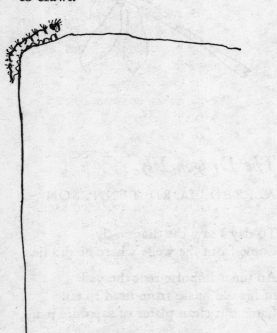

Bee

GEORGE BARKER

I buzz, I buzz, I buzz
because I am a Bee,
I never rest
in my own nest
except when I've
filled up a hive
with *excelicious* Honey,
From West Ealing
to Darjeeling
no other creature can
produce one jot
or tiny spot
of my divine confection:
no, not for love
or health or wealth
no, sir, not even for money
can any factory
make satisfactory
natural Norfolk honey.
From this you see
that I, the Bee,
by natural selection
am cleverer than
machines or man
and very near perfection.

Butterfly

D. H. LAWRENCE

Butterfly, the wind blows sea-ward, strong beyond the
    garden wall!
Butterfly, why do you settle on my shoe, and sip the dirt
    on my shoe,
Lifting your veined wings, lifting them? big white
    butterfly!

Already it is October, and the wind blows strong to the
    sea
from the hills where snow must have fallen, the wind is
    polished with snow.

Here is the garden, with red geraniums, it is warm, it is
    warm
but the wind blows strong to sea-ward, white butterfly,
    content on my shoe!

Will you go, will you go from my warm house?
Will you climb on your big soft wings, black-dotted,
as up an invisible rainbow, an arch
till the wind slides you sheer from the arch-crest
and in a strange level fluttering you go out to sea-ward,
    white speck!

Farewell, farewell, lost soul!
you have melted in the crystalline distance,
it is enough! I saw you vanish into air.

Bees in August

ROY FULLER

It's rather unfair they should not only smell
But gobble the lavender blossom as well.

Four Feet

Furry Bear

A. A. MILNE

If I were a bear
  And a big bear too,
I shouldn't much care
  If it froze or snew;
I wouldn't much mind
  If it snowed or friz —
I'd be all fur-lined
  With a coat like his!

For I'd have fur boots and a brown fur wrap,
And brown fur knickers and a big fur cap.
I'd have a fur muffle-ruff to cover my jaws,
And brown fur mittens on my big brown paws.
With a big brown furry-down up on my head,
I'd sleep all winter in a big fur bed.

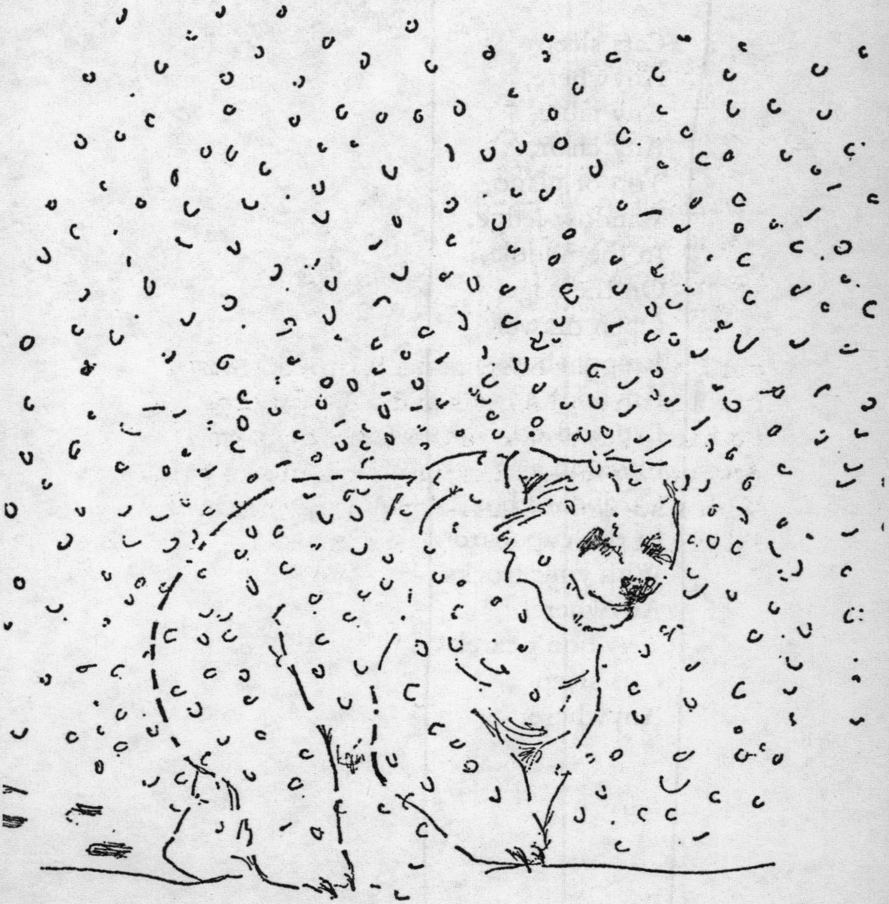

Cats

ELEANOR FARJEON

Cats sleep
Anywhere,
Any table,
Any chair,
Top of piano,
Window-ledge,
In the middle,
On the edge,
Open drawer,
Empty shoe,
Anybody's
Lap will do,
Fitted in a
Cardboard box,
In the cupboard
With your frocks
Anywhere!
They don't care!
Cats sleep
Anywhere.

An Otter

TED HUGHES

Underwater eyes, an eel's
Oil of water body, neither fish nor beast is the otter:
Four-legged yet water-gifted, to outfish fish;
With webbed feet and long ruddering tail
And a round head like an old tomcat.

Brings the legend of himself
From before wars or burials, in spite of hounds and
    vermin-poles;
Does not take root like the badger. Wanders, cries;
Gallops along land he no longer belongs to;
Re-enters the water by melting.

Of neither water nor land. Seeking
Some world lost when first he dived, that he cannot come
    at since,
Takes his changed body into the holes of lakes;
As if blind, cleaves the stream's push till he licks
The pebbles of the source, from sea.

To sea crosses in three nights
Like a king in hiding. Crying to the old shape of the
    starlit land,
Over sunken farms where the bats go round,
Without answer. Till light and birdsong come
Walloping up roads with the milk wagon.

Cows

JAMES REEVES

Half the time they munched the grass, and all the time
  they lay
Down in the water-meadows, the lazy month of May,
      A-chewing,
      A-mooing,
      To pass the hours away.

      "Nice weather," said the brown cow,
      "Ah," said the white.
      "Grass is very tasty,"
      "Grass is all right."

Half the time they munched the grass, and all the time
  they lay
Down in the water-meadows, the lazy month of May,
      A-chewing,
      A-mooing,
      To pass the hours away.

      "Rain coming," said the brown cow,
      "Ah," said the white.
      "Flies is very tiresome."
      "Flies bite."

Half the time they munched the grass, and all the time they lay
Down in the water-meadows, the lazy month of May,
        A-chewing,
        A-mooing,
        To pass the hours away.

"Time to go," said the brown cow,
"Ah," said the white.
"Nice chat." "Very pleasant."
" 'Night." " 'Night."

33

The Monster

EDWARD LOWBRY

A monster who lives in Loch Ness
Is ten thousand years old, more or less:
He's asleep all the time –
Which is hardly a crime:
If he weren't, we'd be in a mess!

Team of Oxen

LOUIS UNTERMEYER

This is earth moving, earth that learned to crawl
Along the glacial wall;
Boulders that rose in their deliberate way
From the raw clay.

Not eagerly, not yet prepared to know
Where they are meant to go,
The damp soil dropping from their sides, they move
In an uncertain groove

Thickly, but pressing on as though their bones
Still feel the push of stones,
And fear to rest themselves lest they remain
Dead earth again.

The Runaway

ROBERT FROST

Once when the snow of the year was beginning to fall,
We stopped by a mountain pasture to say "Whose colt?"
A little Morgan had one forefoot on the wall,
The other curled at his breast. He dipped his head
And snorted to us. And then he had to bolt.
We heard the miniature thunder where he fled,
And we saw him, or thought we saw him, dim and grey,
Like a shadow against the curtain of falling flakes.
"I think the little fellow's afraid of the snow.
He isn't winter-broken. It isn't play
With the little fellow at all. He's running away.
I doubt if even his mother could tell him, 'Sakes,
It's only weather.' He'd think she didn't know!
Where is his mother? He can't be out alone!"
And now he comes again with clatter of stone,
And mounts the wall again with whited eyes
And all his tail that isn't hair up straight.
He shudders his coat as if to throw off flies.
"Whoever it is that leaves him out so late,
When other creatures have gone to stall and bin,
Ought to be told to come and take him in."

The Rhinoceros

OGDEN NASH

The rhino is a homely beast,
For human eyes he's not a feast,
But you and I will never know
Why nature chose to make him so.
Farewell, farewell, you old rhinoceros,
I'll stare at something less prepocerous!

Cat

J. R. R. TOLKIEN

The fat cat on the mat
　　may seem to dream
of nice mice that suffice
　　for him, or cream;
but he free, maybe,
　　walks in thought
unbowed, proud, where loud
　　roared and fought
his kin, lean and slim,
　　or deep in den
in the East feasted on beasts
　　and tender men.

The giant lion with iron
　　claw in paw,
and huge ruthless tooth
　　in gory jaw;
the pard dark-starred
　　fleet upon feet,
that oft soft from aloft
　　leaps on his meat
where woods loom in gloom –
　　far now they be,
　　fierce and free,
　　and tamed is he;
but fat cat on the mat
kept as a pet,
he does not forget.

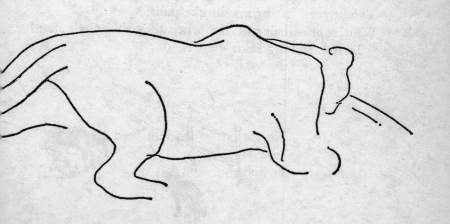

A Sheep Fair

THOMAS HARDY

The day arrives of the autumn fair,
　　And torrents fall,
Though sheep in throngs are gathered there,
　　Ten thousand all,
Sodden, with hurdles round them reared:
And, lot by lot, the pens are cleared,
And the auctioneer wrings out his beard,
And wipes his book, bedrenched and smeared,
And rakes the rain from his face with the edge of his hand,
　　As torrents fall.

The wool of the ewes is like a sponge
　　With the daylong rain:
Jammed tight, to turn, or lie, or lunge,
　　They strive in vain.
Their horns are soft as finger-nails,
Their shepherds reek against the rails,
The tied dogs soak with tucked-in tails,
The buyers' hat-brims fill like pails,
Which spill small cascades when they shift their stand
　　In the daylong rain.

Postscript

Time has trailed lengthily since met
   At Pummery Fair
Those panting thousands in their wet
   And woolly wear:
And every flock long since has bled,
And all the dripping buyers have sped,
And the hoarse auctioneer is dead,
Who "Going – going!" so often said,
As he consigned to doom each meek, mewed band
   At Pummery Fair.

Hedgehog

MILES GIBSON

no one
remembers it
crossing the road

it was – simply – there

armed to the teeth
ugly with fleas
it grunted
in the morning light

and curled up
like a mine

just waiting

for someone
to step out of line

The Tin Frog

RUSSELL HOBAN

I have hopped, when properly wound up, the whole
    length
Of the hallway; once hopped halfway down the stairs, and
    fell,
Since then the two halves of my tin have been awry; my
    strength
Is not quite what it used to be; I do not hop so well.

The Dog

OGDEN NASH

The truth I do not stretch or shove
When I state the dog is full of love.
I've also proved, by actual test,
A wet dog is the lovingest.

The Pig

SPIKE MILLIGAN

A very rash young lady pig
(They say she was a smasher)
    Suddenly ran
    Under a van –
Now she's a gammon rasher.

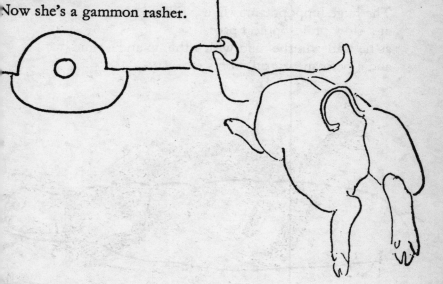

The Hippopotamus

JACK PRELUTSKY

The huge hippopotamus hasn't a hair
on the back of his wrinkly hide;
he carries the bulk of his prominent hulk
rather loosely assembled inside.

The huge hippopotamus lives without care
at a slow philosophical pace,
as he wades in the mud with a thump and a thud
and a permanent grin on his face.

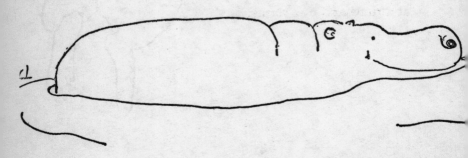

The King

DOUGLAS LIVINGSTONE

Old Tawny's mane is moth-
eaten now, a balding monk's tonsure
and his fluid thigh muscles flop
slack as an exhausted boxer's;

Creaks a little and is
just a fraction under fast (he's lame)
in those last short lethal rushes
at the slim white-eyed winging game;

Can catch them still of course,
the horny old claws combing crimson
from the velvet flanks in long scores,
here in the game-park's environs;

Each year, panting heavily,
manages with aged urbanity
to smile full-faced and yellowly
at a thousand box cameras.

The Toads' Chorus

RUMER GODDEN

The Toads' choir will never tire
aspiring to give delight.
Koak, Koak, croaketty, croak,
every note is right.
I and all the other fellows in our cravats of bilious yellow
Clog, grog, sit on a log, sing on a log all night.
Brekekekekekekek. This is our quarterdeck.
Lumpkin, Bumpkin, Mumkin, Tumpkin, Pumpkin
    nightly cry.
Brekekekekekekek. Swell our stomach and neck.
Odkin, Bodkin, Didkin, Pod and I.
Eyes host to a sadness ghost,
mouth that is post-box wide.
Quick, lick, clicketty click,
insects are flicked inside.
Skin in folds and wrinkled, crinkled,

clammy cold and spot besprinkled.
Ugh! Glug! Slimed as a slug, slimed as a slug our tribe.
Brekekekekekek. All on our quarterdeck.
Muffin, Stuffin, Huffin, Chuffin, Puffin nightly cry.
Jerkin, Perkin, Firkin, Ghurk and I
Call us hideous
venomous it's a lie.
We spurt a villainous squirt
only would hurt a fly.
I and all the other fellows work our cheeks and throats
  like bellows.
Brekekekekekek. Brekekekekekek.
Stop! Hop! Flippetty flip!
          Plop-plop-plop-plop!
              Goodbye!

The Yak

HILAIRE BELLOC

As a friend to the children, commend me the yak;
You will find it exactly the thing:
It will carry and fetch, you can ride on its back,
Or lead it about with a string.

The Tartar who dwells in the plains of Tibet
(A desolate region of snow),
Has for centuries made it a nursery pet,
And surely the Tartar should know!

Then tell your papa where the yak can be got,
And if he is awfully rich,
He will buy you the creature – or else he will not.
I cannot be positive which.

The Mad Yak

GREGORY CORSO

I am watching them churn the last milk
        they'll ever get from me.
They are waiting for me to die;
They want to make buttons out of my bones.
Where are my sisters and brothers?
That tall monk there, loading my uncle,
        he has a new cap.
And that idiot student of his —
I never saw that muffler before.
Poor uncle, he lets them load him.
How sad he is, how tired!
I wonder what they'll do with his bones?
And that beautiful tail!
How many shoelaces will they make of that!

The Galloping Cat

STEVIE SMITH

Oh I am a cat that likes to
Gallop about doing good
So
One day when I was
Galloping about doing good, I saw
A Figure in the path; I said:
Get off! (Be-
cause
I am a cat that likes to
Gallop about doing good)
But he did not move, instead
He raised his hand as if
To land me a cuff
So I made to dodge so as to
Prevent him bringing it orf,
Un-for-tune-ately I slid
On a banana skin
Some Ass had left instead
Of putting in the bin. So
His hand caught me on the cheek
I tried
To lay his arm open from wrist to elbow
With my sharp teeth
Because I am
A cat that likes to gallop about doing good.

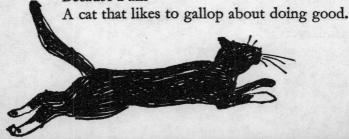

Would you believe it?
He wasn't there
My teeth met nothing but air,
But a Voice said: Poor cat,
(Meaning me) and a soft stroke
Came on me head
Since when I have been bald.
I regard myself as
A martyr to doing good.
Also I heard a swoosh
As of wings, and saw
A halo shining at the height of
Mrs Gubbin's backyard fence,
So I thought: What's the good
Of galloping about doing good
When angels stand in the path
And do not do as they should
Such as having an arm to be bitten off.
All the same I
Intend to go on being
A cat that likes to
Gallop about doing good
So
With my bald head I go,
Chopping the untidy flowers down, to and fro,
An' scooping up the grass to show
Underneath

The cinderpath of wrath
Ha ha ha ha, ho,
Angels aren't the only who do not know
What's what and that
Galloping about doing good
Is a full-time job
That needs
An experienced eye of earthly
Sharpness, worth I dare say
(If you'll forgive a personal note)
A good deal more
Than all that skyey stuff
Of angels that make so bold as
To pity a cat like me that
Gallops about doing good.

Alligator

SPIKE MILLIGAN

From Sydney Zoo
An Alligator
Was put on board
A flying freighter.
He ate the pilot
And the navigator
Then asked for more,
With mashed potater.

Soliloquy of a Tortoise on Revisiting the Lettuce Beds after an Interval of One Hour While Supposed to be in a Clump of Blue Hollyhocks

E. V. RIEU

One cannot have enough
Of this delicious stuff!

The Toaster

WILLIAM JAY SMITH

A silver-scaled Dragon with jaws flaming red
Sits at my elbow and toasts my bread.
I hand him fat slices, and then, one by one,
He hands them back when he sees they are done.

Earthy Anecdote

WALLACE STEVENS

Every time the bucks went clattering
Over Oklahoma
A firecat bristled in the way.

Wherever they went,
They went clattering,
Until they swerved
In a swift, circular line
To the right,
Because of the firecat.

Or until they swerved
In a swift, circular line
To the left,
Because of the firecat.

The bucks clattered.
The firecat went leaping,
To the right, to the left,
And
Bristled in the way.

Later, the firecat closed his bright eyes
And slept.

Giraffe

CARSON McCULLERS

At the zoo I saw: A long-necked, velvety Giraffe
Whose small head, high above the strawy, zooy smells
Seemed to be dreaming.
Was she dreaming of African jungles and African plains
That she would never see again?

Two Feet

The Ostrich

OGDEN NASH

The ostrich roams the great Sahara.
Its mouth is wide, its neck is narra.
It has such long and lofty legs,
I'm glad it sits to lay its eggs.

The Blackbird

HUMBERT WOLFE

In the far corner,
Close by the swings,
Every morning
A blackbird sings.

His bill's so yellow,
His coat's so black,
That he makes a fellow
Whistle back.

Ann, my daughter,
Thinks that he
Sings for us two
Especially.

The Silver Swan

ANONYMOUS

The silver swan, who living had no note,
When death approached, unlocked her silent throat,
Leaning her breast against the reedy shore,
There sung her first and last and sung no more:
Farewell, all joys! O death, come close my eyes;
More geese than swans now live, more fools than wise.

The Eagle

ALFRED, LORD TENNYSON

He clasps the crag with crooked hands;
Close to the sun in lonely lands,
Ring'd with the azure world, he stands.

The wrinkled sea beneath him crawls;
He watches from his mountain walls,
And like a thunderbolt he falls.

The Mirror

A. A. MILNE

Between the woods the afternoon
Is fallen in a golden swoon.
The sun looks down from quiet skies
To where a quiet water lies,
   And silent trees stoop down to trees.
And there I saw a white swan make
Another white swan in the lake;
And, breast to breast, both motionless,
They waited for the wind's caress . . .
   And all the water was at ease.

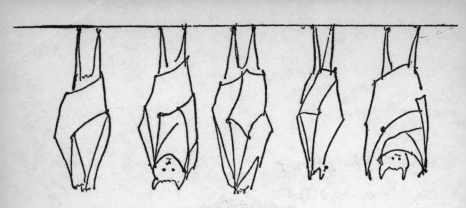

The Bat

THEODORE ROETHKE

By day the bat is cousin to the mouse.
He likes the attic of an ageing house.

His fingers make a hat about his head.
His pulse beat is so slow we think him dead.

He loops in crazy figures half the night
Among the trees that face the corner light.

But when he brushes up against a screen,
We are afraid of what our eyes have seen:

For something is amiss or out of place
When mice with wings can wear a human face.

The Red Cockatoo

PO CHU-I

translated by Arthur Waley

Sent as a present from Annam —
A red cockatoo.
Coloured like the peach-tree blossom,
Speaking with the speech of men.
And they did to it what is always done
To the learned and eloquent.
They took a cage with stout bars
And shut it up inside.

The Sparrowhawk

RUSSELL HOBAN

Wings like pistols flashing at his sides,
Marked, above the meadow runaway tides,
Galloping, galloping with an easy rein.
Below, the field mouse, where the shadow glides,
Holds fast the purse of his life, and hides.

The Caged Bird in Springtime

JAMES KIRKUP

What can it be,
This curious anxiety?
It is as if I wanted
To fly away from here.

But how absurd!
I have never flown in my life,
And I do not know
What flying means, though I have heard,
Of course, something about it.

Why do I peck the wires of this little cage?
It is the only nest I have ever known.
But I want to build my own,
High in the secret branches of the air.

I cannot quite remember how
It is done, but I know
That what I want to do
Cannot be done here.

I have all I need –
Seed and water, air and light.
Why then, do I weep with anguish,
And beat my head and my wings
Against those sharp wires, while the children
Smile at each other, saying: "Hark how he sings"?

The Cock

WILLIAM WORDSWORTH

from An Evening Walk

Sweetly ferocious, round his native walks,
Pride of his sister-wives, the monarch stalks;
Spur-clad his nervous feet, and firm his tread;
A crest of purple tops the warrior's head.
Bright sparks his black and rolling eyeball hurls
Afar, his tail he closes and unfurls;
On tiptoe reared, he strains his clarion throat,
Threatened by faintly-answering farms remote:
Again with his shrill voice the mountain rings,
While, flapped with conscious pride, resound his wings!

The Crow

RUSSELL HOBAN

Flying loose and easy, where does he go
Swaggering in the sky, what does he know,
Why is he laughing, the carrion crow?
Why is he shouting, why won't he sing,
How did he steal, whom will he bring
Loves of blue heaven under each wing?

The Duck

OGDEN NASH

Behold the duck.
It does not cluck.
A cluck it lacks.
It quacks.
It is specially fond
Of a puddle or pond.
When it dines or sups,
It bottoms ups.

. . . and none

Snail

JOHN DRINKWATER

Snail upon the wall,
Have you got at all
Anything to tell
About your shell?

Only this, my child –
When the wind is wild,
Or when the sun is hot,
It's all I've got.

The Serpent

THEODORE ROETHKE

There was a Serpent who had to sing.
There was. There was.
He simply gave up Serpenting.
Because. Because.
He didn't like his Kind of Life;
He couldn't find a proper Wife;
He was a Serpent with a soul;
He got no Pleasure down his Hole.
And so, of course, he had to Sing,
And Sing he did, like Anything!
The Birds, they were, they were Astounded;
And various Measures Propounded
To stop the Serpent's Awful Racket:

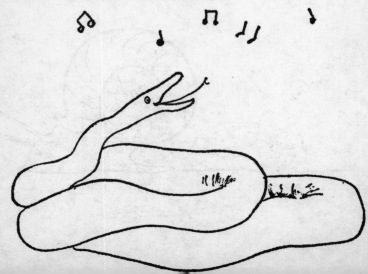

They bought a Drum. He wouldn't Whack it.
They sent – you always send – to Cuba
And got a Most Commodious Tuba;
They got a Horn, they got a Flute,
But Nothing would suit.
He said, "Look Birds, all this is futile:
I do *not* like to Bang or Tootle."
And then he cut loose with a Horrible Note
That practically split the Top of his Throat.
"You see," he said, with a Serpent's Leer,
"I'm serious about my Singing Career!"
And the Woods Resounded with many a Shriek
As the Birds flew off to the End of Next Week.

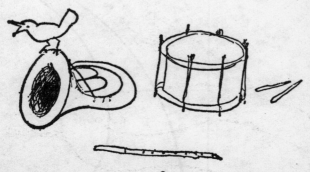

Seal Lullaby

RUDYARD KIPLING

Oh! hush thee, my baby, the night is behind us,
And black are the waters that sparkled so green.
The moon, o'er the combers, looks downward to find us
At rest in the hollows that rustle between.
Where billow meets billow, there soft be thy pillow;
Ah, weary wee flipperling, curl at thy ease!
The storm shall not wake thee, nor sharks overtake thee,
Asleep in the arms of the slow-swinging seas.

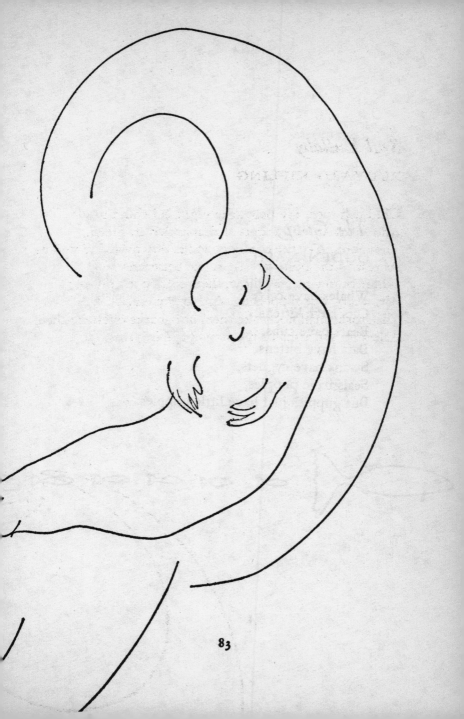

The Guppy

OGDEN NASH

Whales have calves,
Cats have kittens,
Bears have cubs,
Bats have bittens.
Swans have cygnets,
Seals have puppies,
But guppies just have little guppies.

Worms and the Wind

CARL SANDBURG

Worms would rather be worms.
Ask a worm and he says, "Who knows what a worm
knows?"
Worms go down and up and over and under.
Worms like tunnels.
When worms talk they talk about the worm world.
Worms like it in the dark.
Neither the sun nor the moon interest a worm.
Zigzag worms hate circle worms.
Curve worms never trust square worms.
Worms know what worms want.
Slide worms are suspicious of crawl worms.
One worm asks another, "How does your belly drag
today?"
A straight worm says, "Why not be straight?"
Worms tired of crawling begin to slither.
Long worms slither farther than short worms.
Middle-sized worms say, "It is nice to be neither long
nor short."
Old worms teach young worms to say, "Don't be sorry
for me unless you have been a worm and lived in worm
places and read worm books."
When worms go to war they dig in, come out again and
fight, dig in again, come out and fight again, dig in
again, and so on.
Worms underground never hear the wind overground
and sometimes they ask, "What is this wind we hear of?"

lines from *Pike*

TED HUGHES

Pike, three inches long, perfect
Pike in all parts, green fingering the gold.
Killers from the egg: the malevolent aged grin.
They dance on the surface among the flies.

Or move, stunned by their own grandeur,
Over a bed of emerald, silhouette
Of submarine delicacy and horror,
A hundred feet long in their world.

In ponds, under the heat-struck lily pads –
Gloom of their stillness:
Logged on last year's black leaves, watching upwards.
Or hung in an amber cavern of weeds.

The jaws' hooked clamp and fangs
Not to be changed at this date;
A life subdued to its instrument;
The gills kneading quietly, and the pectorals.

The Sailor and the Seal

RUMER GODDEN

When the seal saw the sailor,
It was astonished but not upset,
It had not learnt the meaning of him
Yet,
But trembling on the verge of his surprise,
It gave him a shy welcome with its eyes;
Its heart was in its eyes, soft, infantile;
Its flanks were agitated all the while.

When the sailor saw the seal,
He grew quiet and tense as steel,
Marking the rare tobacco-coloured hide
That wrapped its plumpness in a sweet cocoon.
He took his moment, not too late or soon,
And forward sprung his barbarous harpoon
Into its undulating side.

The seal no longer sees the sailor.
The sailor thinks he has the seal.

. . . and man

Wilderness

CARL SANDBURG

There is a wolf in me . . . fangs pointed for tearing
gashes . . . a red tongue for raw meat . . . and
the hot lapping of blood – I keep this wolf
because the wilderness gave it to me and the
wilderness will not let it go.

There is a fox in me . . . a silver-grey fox . . . I
sniff and guess . . . I pick things out of the
wind and air . . . I nose in the dark night and
take sleepers and eat them and hide the feathers
. . . I circle and loop and double-cross.

There is a hog in me . . . a snout and a belly . . . a
machinery for eating and grunting . . . a
machinery for sleeping satisfied in the sun – I
got this too from the wilderness and the
wilderness will not let it go.

There is a fish in me . . . I know I came from
salt-blue water-gates . . . I scurried with shoals
of herring . . . I blew waterspouts with porpoises
. . . before land was . . . before the water went
down . . . before Noah . . . before the first
chapter of Genesis.

There is a baboon in me . . . clambering-clawed
. . . dog-faced . . . yawping a galoot's* hunger
. . . hairy under the armpits . . . here are the
hawk-eyed hankering men . . . here are the

blonde and blue-eyed women . . . here they
hide curled asleep waiting . . . ready to snarl
and kill . . . ready to sing and give milk . . .
waiting – I keep the baboon because the
wilderness says so.

There is an eagle in me and a mockingbird . . .
and the eagle flies among the Rocky Mountains
of my dreams and fights among the Sierra crags
of what I want . . . and the mockingbird
warbles in the early forenoon before the dew
is gone, warbles in the underbrush of my
Chattanoogas of hope, gushes over the blue
Ozark foothills of my wishes – And I got the
eagle and the mockingbird from the wilderness.

O, I got a zoo, I got a menagerie, inside my ribs,
under my bony head, under my red-valve
heart – and I got something else: it is a man-
child heart, a woman-child heart: it is a father
and mother and lover: it came from God-
Knows-Where: it is going to God-Knows-
Where – For I am the keeper of the zoo: I
say yes and no: I sing and kill and work: I
am a pal of the world: I came from the
wilderness.

* uncouth fellow

Index of Authors and Poems

ANONYMOUS
A centipede   16
The Silver Swan   65

BARKER, GEORGE
Bee   23

BELLOC, HILAIRE
The Scorpion   13
The Yak   50

BERNOS DE GASZTOLD,
   CARMEN
The Centipede   20

BROWNJOHN, ALAN
Spider   11

CORSO, GREGORY
The Mad Yak   51

DRINKWATER, JOHN
Snail   79

FARJEON, ELEANOR
Cats   30

FROST, ROBERT
Fireflies in the Garden   18
The Runaway   36

FULLER, ROY
Bees in August   25

GIBSON, MILES
Hedgehog   42

GODDEN, RUMER
The Centipede (as translator)
   20
The Sailor and the Seal   88
The Toads' Chorus   48

HARDY, THOMAS
A Sheep Fair   40

HOBAN, RUSSELL
The Crow   75
The Sparrowhawk   71
The Tin Frog   43

HUGHES, TED
An Otter   31
lines from Pike   86

KEATS, JOHN
On the Grasshopper and
   Cricket   14

KIPLING, RUDYARD
The Butterfly That Stamped
   12
Seal Lullaby   82

KIRKUP, JAMES
The Caged Bird in   72
   Springtime

LAWRENCE, D. H.
Butterfly   24

LIVINGSTONE, DOUGLAS
The King   47

LOWBRY, EDWARD
The Monster   34

MARQUIS, DON
the honey bee   19

MILLIGAN, SPIKE
Alligator   55
The Pig   45

MILNE, A. A.
Furry Bear   28
The Mirror   67

MCCULLERS, CARSON
Giraffe   59

NASH, OGDEN
The Dog   44
The Duck   76
The Guppy   84
The Ostrich   63
The Rhinoceros   37

PO CHU-I
The Red Cockatoo   70

PRELUTSKY, JACK
The Hippopotamus   46

REEVES, JAMES
Cows   32

RIEU, E. V.
Soliloquy of a Tortoise   56

ROETHKE, THEODORE
The Bat   68
The Serpent   80

SANDBURG, CARL
Wilderness   90
Worms and the Wind   85

SERRAILLIER, IAN
The Tickle Rhyme   22

SHANNON, MONICA
Only my Opinion   17

SMITH, WILLIAM JAY
The Toaster   57

SMITH, STEVIE
The Galloping Cat   52

STEVENS, WALLACE
Earthy Anecdote   58

TENNYSON, ALFRED LORD
The Dragon-Fly   21
The Eagle   66

TOLKIEN, J. R. R.
Cat   38

TRADITIONAL AMERICAN
Way Down South   15

UNTERMEYER, LOUIS
Team of Oxen   35

WALEY, ARTHUR (as
  translator)
The Red Cockatoo   70

WOLFE, HUMBERT
The Blackbird   64

WORDSWORTH, WILLIAM
The Cock   74

Acknowledgements

Particular thanks are due to Rumer Godden for her help and support. The Editor gratefully acknowledges permission to reprint copyright material to the following: Faber & Faber for Bee from The Alphabetical Animal Zoo by George Barker; Alfred A. Knopf Inc. and Gerald Duckworth & Co. Ltd for The Scorpion and The Yak from Cautionary Verses by Hilaire Belloc; the Trustees of the Hardy Estate and Macmillan, London and Basingstoke for A Sheep Fair by Thomas Hardy; Macmillan, London and Basingstoke and The Viking Press for the Centipede from Beasts' Choir by Carmen Bernos de Gaszcold, translated by Rumer Godden; Macmillan, London and Basingstoke and Charles Scribner's Sons for Spider from Brownjohn's Beasts by Alan Brownjohn; the author's representatives, Samuel French Ltd, for The Snail by John Drinkwater; The Oxford University Press and David Higham Associates Ltd for Cats from Silver Sand and Snow by Eleanor Farjeon; Holt, Rinehart & Winston Inc. for Fireflies in the Garden and The Runaway by Robert Frost; Andre Deutsch for Bees in August from Seen Grandpa Lately? by Roy Fuller; Methuen & Co. Ltd, as publishers, and Miles Gibson for Hedgehog from The Guilty Bystander by Miles Gibson, copyright 1970; Rumer Godden and Curtis Brown Ltd for the previously unpublished Toads' Chorus and The Sailor and the Seal by Rumer Godden; World's Work Ltd and Grosset & Dunlap Inc. for The Crow, The Sparrowhawk, and The Tin Frog from The Pedalling Man and Other Poems by Russell Hoban; Faber & Faber Ltd and Harper & Row, New York for An Otter and lines from Pike from Lupercal by Ted Hughes; Macmillan, London and Basingstoke, and Doubleday & Co. Inc., New York, and The National Trust for The Butterfly That Stamped and Lullaby of a Seal from The Definitive Edition of Rudyard Kipling's Verse; Laurence Pollinger Ltd, The Estate of the late Mrs Frieda Lawrence and The Viking Press Inc. of New York for The Butterfly from The Complete Poems of D. H. Lawrence published by William Heinemann Ltd; Edward Lowbury for The Monster from Green Magic by Edward Lowbury published by Chatto & Windus Ltd; Faber & Faber Ltd and Doubleday & Co. Inc., New York, for lines from archi and mehitabel by Don Marquis; Dennis Dobson Publishers for Alligator and The Pig from A Book of Milliganimals by Spike Milligan; The Estate of A. A. Milne, Curtis Brown Ltd London on behalf of the Pooh Properties, the Canadian publishers McClelland & Stewart, Toronto, and E. P. Dutton for Furry Bear from Now We Are Six and The Mirror from When We Were Very Young by A. A. Milne; Carson McCullers, Jonathan Cape Ltd and Houghton Mifflin Co. for Giraffe from Sweet As A Pickle and Clean As A Pig by Carson McCullers; The Estate of the late Ogden Nash, J. M. Dent & Sons, and Curtis Brown, New York, for The Dog from Everyone But Thee and Me, The Guppy from Versus, and The Duck, The Ostrich and The Rhinoceros from You Can't Get There From Here by Ogden Nash; Oxford University Press for Cows from The Blackbird in the Lilac by James Reeves, copyright 1952; Richard Rieu for Soliloquy of a Tortoise on Revisiting the Lettuce Beds after an Interval of One Hour While Supposed to be in a Clump of Blue Hollyhocks by E. V. Rieu; Faber & Faber Ltd and Doubleday & Co. Inc., New York, for The Bat and The Serpent from The Collected Poems of Theodore Roethke; Holt, Rinehart & Winston Inc. for Wilderness from Cornhuskers by Carl Sandburg; Harcourt Brace Jovanovitch Inc. for Worms and the Wind from Complete Poems, copyright 1950 by Carl Sandburg; Ian Serraillier for The Tickle Rhyme from The Tale of the Monster Horse by Ian Serraillier published by the Oxford University Press; Doubleday & Co. Inc., the publisher, for Only My Opinion from Goose Grass Rhymes by Monica Shannon, copyright 1930; William Jay Smith for The Toaster from Laughing Time published by Atlantic-Little, copyright William Jay Smith 1955; James McGibbon as Executor, Allen Lane as publisher, and the Oxford University Press for The Galloping Cat from The Collected Poems of Stevie Smith; Faber & Faber Ltd and Alfred A. Knopf Inc. for Earthy Anecdote from Collected Poems of Wallace Stevens; George Allen & Unwin (Publishers) Ltd and Houghton Mifflin Co. for Cat from The Adventures of Tom Bombadil by J. R. R. Tolkien; Harcourt Brace Jovanovitch Inc. for Team of Oxen from Burning Bush by Louis Untermeyer, copyright 1928, renewed 1956 by Louis Untermeyer; Miss Ann Wolfe for The Blackbird from Kensington Gardens by Humbert Wolfe.

Every effort has been made to trace the owners of the copyright material in this book. It is the Editor's belief that all necessary permissions have been obtained, but in the case of any question arising as to the use of any material, the Editor will be pleased to make the necessary corrections in future editions of the book.